The Clever Teens' Guide to

Nazi

Germany

Felix Rhodes

Other titles in the series:

The Clever Teens' Guide to

Nazi Germany

Felix Rhodes

Table of Contents

Post-Great War

On November 11, 1918, World War One came to an end. After four long years and four months, Germany had been defeated. Although Germany itself had not been invaded, the country was devastated by poverty and hunger. To add to its woes, Germany, like most European nations, was swept by the Spanish Flu pandemic. The nation was on its knees. On November 10, the day before Germany's surrender, the German Kaiser, Wilhelm II, abdicated.

Peace brought relief but there was also anger – anger that the politicians, not the military leadership, had so easily surrendered to France and Great Britain. One German corporal, at the time recuperating in hospital from a gas attack, spoke for many when, in his memoirs, he remembered sobbing into his pillow on hearing the news of Germany's defeat. The name of this particular corporal was Adolf Hitler.

Following Wilhelm II's abdication, Germany fell into a state of chaos. Communists and the far right fought on the streets of Berlin and other cities throughout the country. A group of communists called the Spartacus League staged a revolt. It failed and 1,200 communists were executed.

Despite the fighting, Germany managed to form a republican government. Berlin was still too chaotic so this new government, headed by President Friedrich Ebert, set itself up in the town of Weimar – the Weimar Republic was born.

Treaty of Versailles

During the first six months of 1919, leaders of the victorious Allied nations convened at the Paris Peace Conference. Between them, they decided on how best to punish the defeated nations and how to make sure the war really was the "war to end all wars". The treaty that dealt with Germany was named the Treaty of Versailles. Its terms were harsh and non-negotiable. Germany lost 13 per cent of her territory, which meant 12 per cent of Germans now lived in a foreign country, and all its colonial possessions in Africa and Asia. The German Rhineland, on the border with France, was to be demilitarized (stripped of an armed presence) and placed under Allied control until 1935. The small but industrially important Saar region was to be governed by Britain and France for fifteen years and its coal (2 million tons a month) exported to France. After fifteen years a plebiscite (or referendum) of the Saar population would be allowed to decide its future.

Germany's army was to be restricted to a token 100,000 men, and its navy to just 15,000 men. She was not permitted to have an air force, nor submarines or tanks.

Then came the financial punishment – the treaty demanded that Germany pay 132 billion gold marks in reparations to compensate "for all damage done to the civilian population of the Allied powers and their property". It was to include raw material, such as coal. The figure shocked and angered Germans who argued that such a sum would bankrupt the nation.

The treaty also made sure that Germany accepted responsibility for having started the war in the first place – the "war guilt clause".

Outraged Germans accused the politicians of not standing up to the Allies and for accepting the terms of the treaty.

The Weimar Republic

The German Workers' Party

Throughout Germany, small political parties sprung up while the communists and right-wingers still fought each other on the streets. In January 1919, a Munich locksmith called Anton Drexler founded a new political party, the German Workers' Party, or to use its German initials – DAP. It had only a handful of members and would undoubtedly have been forgotten by history if, on September 12, 1919, it hadn't been for the unexpected arrival of Adolf Hitler.

Hitler had joined the German army right at the start of the war in August 1914. He was promoted to the rank of corporal but never managed to go any higher. He spent most of the war working as a messenger. He was twice wounded and twice awarded medals for bravery. In 1919, he was still working for the army, tasked with keeping an eye on new political groups based in Munich. And so Hitler arrived at a meeting being chaired by Drexler. Hitler got himself into an argument with a guest speaker and, in doing so, impressed Drexler who promptly invited Hitler to join his party.

Adolf Hitler (far right) during the First World War.

As a member of DAP, Hitler began giving speeches – and found he was good at it. He spoke of the "November criminals" – the Bolshevik and Jewish politicians deemed responsible for Germany's defeat in November 1918 – and attacked the Versailles Treaty and its injustices. His fiery speeches attracted more and more people. Drexler was

certainly impressed. Thanks to his newest recruit, his party
was becoming a force to be reckoned with.

The National Socialist German Workers' Party

On February 24, 1920, the party changed its name from
the German Workers Party to the National Socialist
German Workers' Party, or NSDAP. More people,
seduced by Hitler, joined the party, including men who,
over the years, would become globally famous – Heinrich
Himmler, Hermann Goring and Rudolph Hess. The party
came up with a manifesto, a list of 25 demands which
included the nullification of the Versailles Treaty, the
expulsion of immigrants, and that German Jews be
stripped of their citizenship. Hitler helped design a new
flag for the party – a black swastika in a white circle on a
red background.

Hitler's speeches certainly drew the crowds – including
the rival communists, determined to disrupt Nazi
meetings. To provide protection and beat up the
communists, the Nazis established its own paramilitary
wing, the *Sturmabteilung*, abbreviated to the SA and
nicknamed the "Brownshirts".

However, not all was well. There were some in the
party who were worried by Hitler's fanaticism and in June

1921, they tried to banish Hitler from the party. Hitler responded by offering to resign. The party leadership, knowing they were nothing without Hitler, begged him to stay. He would stay, said Hitler, but only as party leader. Hence, on July 28, 1921, Anton Drexler stepped aside, becoming the party's "honourary president". Adolf Hitler was now NSDAP's new chairman. He insisted on being called *Fuhrer*, "leader", and introduced the raised arm "Hitler salute".

Meanwhile, the German government was already behind in its reparation payments. In 1923, France decided to extract reparations by direct means, by occupying the industrial Rhineland. German workers reacted by going on strike and the German government responded by printing more money in order to continue paying the striking workers. Germany was already suffering from severe inflation. Simply printing more money made the situation worse. Soon prices spiralled out of control, resulting in Germany's period of hyperinflation. People lost their lifesavings overnight. Workers were collecting suitcases full of money as wages. Fighting broke-out in cities throughout the country. Communists fought nationalists; all sought to bring down the government.

The Munich Putsch

With the nation teetering on the brink of civil war, Hitler felt the time was ripe to stage an uprising. The revolt was to take place in Munich, ahead of a "march on Berlin". On November 8, 1923, Munich's top officials were meeting in a beer hall when Hitler and his entourage, wielding guns and shouting "Heil Hitler", took over the meeting.

Preparing for the Munich Putsch, November 1923.
German Federal Archive.

In the early hours, as the Nazis headed through the town, their way was blocked by police. A gunfight ensued and four police officers and sixteen Nazis were killed.

Hitler, falling to the ground, dislocated his shoulder before being arrested.

The Munich *Putsch* had failed.

Hitler was put on trial where, in front of weak and sympathetic judges, he was able to deliver his speeches. Almost overnight, Hitler had become a household name throughout Germany.

Hitler never denied the charges. His sentence of five years was considered very light.

Mein Kampf

While in prison, Hitler dictated to Rudolph Hess his autobiographical book, *Mein Kampf* ("My Struggle"). The book sets out Hitler's political thinking, his extreme anti-Semitism, and his belief in racial purity and *Lebensraum*, "living space". The "Aryan" race, as he saw it, stood at the peak of human civilization; while the Jewish "race" was the lowest. Germany, he wrote, needed more living space. This space was to be found east of Germany, an area populated by the inferior Slavs. Once Germany had claimed their "rightful" territory in the east, the Slavs, in Hitler's vision, were to become slaves to their German masters.

Hitler served only eight months of his five year sentence. On his release, he took up the reins of his party, promising that from then on the Nazi party would respect the legal process.

The mid to late 1920s could be considered the Weimar Republic's "golden years". In 1924, a US financier and future vice president, Charles Dawes, came up with a plan in which Germany would resume reparation payments but at a much more manageable level and in which the US would lend Germany money. The Dawes Plan also stipulated that the French withdraw from the Ruhr. It did. With US loans, economically, politically and socially, things calmed down in Germany. In March 1925, the 77-year-old Paul von Hindenburg, hero of the Great War, was elected president. Germany was inducted into the League of Nations, a symbolic gesture to show that Germany was being welcomed back into the international arena.

Hitler Youth

From as early as 1922 there had been a youth element to the SA and in July 1926, the Hitler Youth (HJ) was founded – aimed at boys aged 14 and upwards. The "German Youth" for boys aged 10 to 14, was founded in 1928, and in 1930, the League of German Girls. Similar to the scouting movement, these youth groups encouraged solidarity and comradeship, and physical and moral fitness.

Hitler wanted German youth to be "as swift as a greyhound, as tough as leather, and as hard as Krupp's steel". In early 1933, just before Hitler came to power, there were some 107,000 HJ members. By the end of the year, the number had risen to 2.3 million. Membership was not compulsory at first but failure to join was certainly frowned upon and parents who "prevented" their children from joining were considered with suspicion. Membership only became compulsory in 1939.

In May 1928, Germany held national elections. The Nazi party won just 2.6 per cent of the vote and gained 12 Reichstag seats. (Joseph Goebbels and Hermann Goring were among the twelve). The Social Democrats, winning almost 30 per cent of the vote, remained in power.

Hitler had begun to tire of the thuggish SA and their leader, Ernst Rohm. Instead, he formed a new security system, a more personalised bodyguard for the party elite – the feared SS. From 1929, the man in charge of the SS was an ex-chicken farmer, and a Hitler devotee – Heinrich Himmler.

In August 1929, the Nazis staged their fourth Party Congress – the venue was the town of Nuremberg. Adorned with swastikas, the rally, drawing vast crowds, proved a huge success for Hitler and his party. Membership continued to grow – from about 17,000 members in 1925 to almost 180,000 in 1929. Such was the strength of the party by 1930, that Hitler appointed various *gauleiters* (district leaders) across the country, ensuring that nowhere was beyond the reach of the party. The new German chancellor, Heinrich Brüning, appointed in March 1930, had reasons to be fearful.

The Great Depression

In 1929, an American banker called Owen D. Young issued a report on Germany's finances in which he suggested that Germany's reparations be cut by 75 per cent payable over a period of 59 years – up to 1988. The Young Plan was adopted but then came "Black Thursday" – October 24, 1929, and the crash of the Wall Street Market in New York. The repercussions were felt across the world, nowhere more so than in Germany, a country dependent on US loans. Following the crash, reparations were suspended for a year and by 1931 dropped altogether. Germany had paid back only an eighth of the original demand. But there was to be no more financial aid from the US. The depression saw unemployment in Germany rapidly increase, reaching 2.5 million by the end of 1930 and to 6 million by 1932, 20 per cent of Germany's workforce.

Unable to command a majority within the Reichstag and with President Hindenburg's approval, Chancellor Brüning began to rule by emergency decree. Then, in September 1930, hoping to improve his support, Brüning called an election.

The 1930 election saw a huge upsurge for the National Socialists. The Social Democrats retained power but their share of the vote dropped to 24.5 per cent, giving them 143 seats in the Reichstag, a loss of ten seats. The Nazis, having come ninth in 1928, finished 1930 as the country's second largest political party, having gained over 18 per cent of the vote and winning 107 seats in the Reichstag (30 seats more than the communists). It was, by any standards, an impressive result.

In the spring of 1932, Adolf Hitler pitted himself against the Paul von Hindenburg in Germany's presidential election. Hindenburg, having been president of Weimar Germany since 1925, wished to retire – he was, after all, 84 years old and not in particularly good health. But such was his loathing for the Nazis and Hitler in particular, that he felt he had no option but to stand. The first round of elections, in March 1932, produced no clear winner. In the second round, Hindenburg won 53 per cent of the vote and so held onto his post. Hitler won 30 per cent of the vote while Ernst Thalmann, head of Germany's communist party, came a poor third. Hindenburg started his new term by sacking Brüning as chancellor and replacing him with Franz von Papen.

Paul von Hindenburg. Library of Congress.

But it was the national elections of July 1932 that really paved the way for Hitler and the National Socialists. Von Papen had minimal support within the Reichstag and, like Brüning before him, hoped an election would remedy the situation. Ahead of election day, Ernst Rohm's SA thugs went on the rampage, intimidating opposing parties and their supporters. The Nazis won 230 seats in 1932 and 37.3 per cent of the vote. It wasn't enough to command a majority and so Von Papen held onto his post as chancellor but now, for the first time, the National Socialist Party was the biggest party in Germany.

There was another election four months later. The Nazi vote fell a little but the party still had enough electoral clout that Hitler, as dictated by the Weimar constitution, should have been appointed chancellor.

The Nazis in Power

Hitler appointed Chancellor

Hindenburg was loath to appoint the former corporal. Franz von Papen, no longer chancellor, believed the Nazis were already a spent force after the dip in the Nazi vote in November 1932 He decided to work with the Nazi leader. He put forward an idea to Hindenburg – the president should appoint Hitler chancellor with Von Papen his vice chancellor where he could control and manipulate Hitler. Hitler, Papen argued, needed to be controlled and this would be far easier with Hitler working inside the government than causing trouble from outside. "In two months," said Papen, "we'll have pushed Hitler into a corner where he can squeal to his heart's content."

Reluctantly, Hindenburg agreed. Von Papen approached Hitler and made his offer. Only three of the 11 other cabinet posts would be filled with Nazis, meaning Von Papen would be able to keep the Nazis in check.

And so on January 30, 1933, Hitler was appointed Chancellor within a coalition government.

Von Papen soon found to his cost that he was unable to control the new chancellor and it was he, not Hitler, who was "pushed into a corner", to become an inconsequential figure.

The Reichstag Fire

Four weeks after his appointment, fate played into Hitler's hands. At 9 p.m. on February 27, 1933, Berlin's Reichstag building was set ablaze. The arsonist was a 24-year-old suspected communist called Marinus van der Lubbe, an unemployed Dutch bricklayer. Van der Lubbe confessed to the crime, insisting he'd acted alone and denying any involvement with the communists.

The following day, President Hindenburg accepted Hitler's request for a decree suspending all political and civil liberties as a "temporary" measure for the "protection of the people and state". The communists, according to Hitler, were attempting a *putsch*, a revolt, and thousands of known communists were arrested, tortured and either murdered or placed in the newly-opened concentration camps for "protective custody". Dachau, near Munich, the first concentration camp, was opened on March 22.

The Reichstag Fire, February 27, 1933.
German Federal Archives.

Marinus van der Lubbe was executed in 1934 but tales persisted even at the time that the Nazis themselves had started the Reichstag Fire. The fire certainly helped Hitler establish his power. The temporary suspension of liberties was never withdrawn and any active opposition to the Nazis was stifled. When, the following month, on March 5, the last parliamentary elections took place, only Hitler, it was claimed, could save Germany from the Jews and communists. The SA intimidated all other parties into silence and the Nazis polled 43.9 per cent of the vote, still not quite enough for a majority but enough to crush any future political resistance.

The Enabling Act

In the event it didn't matter that Hitler still hadn't achieved a majority within the Reichstag – because he simply did away with it.

He proposed the Enabling Act in order to allow him greater time to deal with the nation's problems, and to dispense with the constitution, the Reichstag and the electoral system. Hitler needed a two-thirds majority in the Reichstag to pass the act. Meeting in Berlin's Opera House, the Reichstag members found themselves surrounded by Hitler's Stormtroopers. Thus intimidated, all but the brave Social Democrats voted for the act by 444 votes to 94. There would be no more free elections nor a constitution to keep Hitler in check. The Reichstag had, in effect, voted away its power.

Very soon, the firm hand of the state was being felt across the country. It became illegal to criticise or "undermine" the government. Those who expressed critical opinions risked being denounced to the new secret police force, the Gestapo. Known and suspected opponents of the regime were sent without trial to the concentration camps. Trade unions were banned (replaced by the German Workers' Front, DAF), their leaders arrested; freedom of the press was curtailed; and by the end of July all other political parties had been declared illegal, leaving only the Nazi party. Germany had, very quickly, become a one-party state with Hitler its dictator.

On May 10, 1933, cities throughout Germany took part in a series of organised book burning ceremonies, labelled "Action against the Un-German Spirit". Thousands of "un-German" books were set alight and destroyed, including works by Ernest Hemingway, D H Lawrence, H G Wells, James Joyce, Leon Tolstoy and the 19th century German Jewish writer, Heinrich Heine. In the 1820s, Heine had famously written, "Where they burn books, they will in the end also burn people".

On November 12, 1933, at the first national elections since the passing of the Enabling Act, the National Socialists won all 661 seats in the Reichstag. Hardly surprising, in that they were the only party standing. On the same day, the people voted in a referendum on whether Germany should remain part of the League of Nations. 95.1 per cent voted to leave.

The "Night of the Long Knives"

A year later, with Hitler's power almost absolute, only the excesses of the SA and their leader, Ernst Rohm, troubled the dictator. The SA maintained their thuggish reputation, while Hitler wanted to have the appearance, at least, of respectability – especially on the international stage. Rohm and the SA felt that Hitler had gone soft and talked of staging a "second revolution" with Rohm the leader of a People's Party. Respectable industrialists and businessmen were alarmed, as was President Hindenburg and the German army. Rohm made no secret of his desire to merge the army with the SA under his command.

In April 1934, Hitler and army chief Werner von Blomberg made a deal: Hitler would ensure Rohm's downfall in return for Blomberg full support.

Hindenburg, threatening to impose martial law, also pressed Hitler into dealing with his unruly SA.

Hindenburg and Hitler, March 1933 (with Blomberg in the middle). German Federal Archives.

On the weekend of June 30 – July 1, 1934, Hitler acted. The SA had gathered for a weekend of fun in a hotel in the village of Bad Wiessee. Members of the SS moved in and had them arrested. Most were executed on the spot, except for Rohm. Hitler took it upon himself to arrest Rohm personally, marching into his hotel room and, brandishing a revolver, yelling, "You're under arrest, you pig".

Rohm was taken to a Munich prison and was murdered the following day.

The "Night of the Long Knives" claimed over 200 victims, including many who had crossed Hitler in the past. Hindenburg was delighted with Hitler's forcefulness while the army, relieved to be freed from its main rival, declared its loyalty to the Fuhrer. All soldiers were now obliged to swear an oath of personal loyalty not to the state but to Hitler himself.

On August 2, 1934, Paul von Hindenburg died. He was 86. Within two hours of Hindenburg's death, Hitler announced that as from that moment the posts of president and chancellor were to be merged, thereby making Hitler both the head of state and the head of government. But, just to make sure, on August 19, the Nazis staged a plebiscite, a referendum, asking whether the German people approved of such a move. 88.1 per cent said yes. Adolf Hitler was now Germany's fully-fledged dictator.

Economy

Hitler set about improving the Germany's economy. A vast network of motorways was constructed, land reclamation schemes introduced, sports stadiums built, the car industry rejuvenated. As a result, unemployment in Germany fell rapidly – from six million in January 1933 to 2.5 million within just two years. But it was rearmament that remained Hitler's economic priority, despite it being strictly prohibited by the Treaty of Versailles.

In a series of speeches, Hitler denounced war while reintroducing conscription (all 21-year-old men were obliged to complete a year's military service) and secretly stepping up Germany's programme of rearmament and militarization.

1934 - 1939

Austria

Hitler turned his mind to his foreign policy ambitions. One of his priorities was to incorporate Austria (the country of his birth) into a "Greater Germany". On July 25, 1934, on Hitler's urging, Austrian Nazis attempted to overthrow the government. Charging into the Austrian chancellery in Vienna, they shot and killed the Austrian chancellor, Engelbert Dollfuss. Vowing to defend Austrian independence and support Dollfuss' replacement, Kurt von Schuschnigg, Italy's fascist leader, Benito Mussolini, warned Hitler against invading Austria, posting Italian soldiers on the Italian-Austrian border just in case.

The Saar

The Saar region, once a part of Germany, had, under the terms of the Versailles Treaty, been administered by the League of Nations for a period of 15 years. The 15 years had passed and so on January 13, 1935, the people of Saar were offered the choice of whether to remain under the control of the League of Nations, to become part of France or be re-united with Germany. The result was an overwhelming 90.3 per cent vote in favour of Germany. It was, for Hitler, a small but significant victory.

The Stresa Front

With Hitler openly declaring his contempt of the Versailles Treaty and its limitations upon German revival, Great Britain, France and Italy met to discuss the situation in the Italian town of Stresa. The resultant "Stresa Front", signed April 14, 1935, announced their determination to uphold Austrian independence, and agreed to stand united against Hitler. But the high ideals of Stresa would start to unravel within a matter of months.

It was Great Britain that first weakened the agreements made at Stresa. In June 1935, just two months after the Stresa signing, Britain and Germany signed a naval agreement. Under the terms of the agreement, Germany would be allowed to have a navy 35 per cent the size of Britain's Royal Navy, and possess an equal amount of submarines. France and Italy were furious – not only did this exceed the naval limit set by Versailles and not only did it undermine the Stresa Front but Britain had failed to consult the French or Italians before going ahead and signing the agreement.

Benito Mussolini and Adolf Hitler in Munich, June 1940.

Mussolini had a rather low opinion of Hitler and, as we have seen, was prepared to stand up to him following the failed coup in Austria. In his desire to have his own colonial empire, Mussolini ordered the invasion of

Abyssinia (now Ethiopia) in October 1935. The local Ethiopians, faced with the might of a modern air force and army, stood little chance. The League of Nations protested and imposed economic sanctions against Italy. Mussolini won his war but at the cost of being ostracised by the leading members of the League of Nations, specifically France and Britain, his co-signatories of the Stresa Front. Instead, he found a greater rapport with Hitler which manifested itself on October 25, 1936, when Italy and Germany signed the first document that bound them to each other, the Rome-Berlin Axis. The Stresa Front was dead.

The Rhineland

An equally challenging situation centred round the Rhineland, which, again under the terms of the Versailles treaty, had been demilitarized. The French presence had come to an end but the state of demilitarization was to remain a permanent feature. But Hitler had other ideas.

On March 7, 1936, Hitler ordered 22,000 German troops into the Rhineland. They were warmly welcomed. Fearing that French soldiers were gathering on the Franco-German border, Hitler almost lost his nerve. Indeed, Blomberg, his army chief, urged him to withdraw his troops. It was a watershed moment. Had France marched against the poorly-equipped Germans, and had France had the backing of the British, the Germans would have had no choice but to withdraw, which would have spelt the end for Hitler. But France didn't react. Nor did Britain. Hitler's bravado paid off. Indeed, many in Britain quietly approved of his actions. After all, the Rhineland was German, thus Hitler, they argued, was merely reclaiming his "own backyard". Hitler's prestige at home, already high, now soared. Meanwhile, he tried to calm his European enemies, declaring, "We have no more territorial claims to make in Europe".

Spanish Civil War

In July 1936, the Spanish Civil War broke out – fought between General Francisco Franco's nationalists and a broad coalition of left-wing affiliations – socialist, communist, republican, anarchist, etc. Joseph Stalin, leader of the Soviet Union, aided the latter while Hitler and Mussolini sent men, equipment and aid to the former. Again, Great Britain and France did nothing. On April 26, 1937, in perhaps the most notorious incident of the Spanish Civil War, the German Luftwaffe bombed the Basque town of Guernica, killing some 500 civilians. It was, for Hitler's air force, a practice run for things to come.

Hitler and Germany's Jews

Germany's Jewish population had suffered at the hands of Hitler's party even before Hitler had been appointed chancellor. But from January 1933, their situation became increasingly more difficult. Jews were beaten up and their homes and businesses vandalised as towns put up signs declaring "Jews not wanted here", actively aiming to become "Jew-free".

On April 7, the National Socialists passed the first of many anti-Semitic laws, which effectively made it illegal for Jews (and political opponents) to serve in the German civil service. Virtually overnight, a Jew could no longer teach or serve as a judge or lawyer. Soon, Jewish doctors were not permitted to treat non-Jewish patients, and the number of Jewish students at schools and university was severely restricted. Over the years, the regime introduced increasingly absurd laws against the Jews, causing Germany's Jews untold hardship and deprivation.

Many in the Jewish population tragically believed the situation would, at some point, improve. Others refused out of principle to leave their homeland. But out of a population of half million Jews in Germany in 1933, about 320,000 had emigrated by 1939.

Nuremberg Rally, 1934. German Federal Archives.

On September 15, 1935, the Nuremberg Race Laws were instituted in which the German state defined "Jewishness". The laws defined whether a person was Jewish according to their ancestry, rather than their religious beliefs and practices. Anybody with at least three Jewish grandparents, or with just two Jewish grandparents but who was religious or married to a Jew, was now deemed wholly Jewish under Nazi law. Everyone categorized as a Jew was stripped of their German citizenship, disenfranchised, and forbidden to marry or to have sexual liaisons with non-Jews. Two Jewish grandparents made you a first degree Mischling, whilst one Jewish grandparent resulted in a second-degree categorization. The Jews were no longer "of German blood".

The degree of state-sponsored anti-Semitism was temporarily toned-down during the summer of 1936 when Berlin hosted the Summer Olympics. The International Olympic Committee had awarded Berlin the Games in 1931, before the Nazis had come to power. Initially, Jews were to be barred from competing but faced with an international outcry, Hitler relented. On August 1, Hitler officially declared the games open. Germany topped the medals' table, winning 89 medals (33 gold), the US came second, Hungary third and Mussolini's Italy fourth with 22 medals (8 gold). But it was the American black athlete, Jesse Owens, who stole the headlines, winning four gold medals, and making a mockery of Hitler's theory of Aryan superiority.On November 25, 1936, Germany signed an anti-communist pact with the empire of Japan, aimed specifically against the Soviet Union. A year later, Italy added its signature. In September 1937, Mussolini paid an official visit to Germany. The Italian dictator was now firmly in Hitler's camp.

In February 1938, Hitler made himself commander of the German army, dismissing Werner von Blomberg. Blomberg had proved to be too old-fashioned for Hitler's liking. Now, with Blomberg out of the way, Hitler could do as he pleased with the army. And it was to Austria he turned his attention.

Anschluss

Hitler's attempts in July 1934 to use Austrian Nazis to stage a coup may have failed but in the intervening four years things had changed. Now, for one thing, he had Mussolini on his side. Indeed, in April 1937, Mussolini informed the Austrian chancellor, Kurt von Schuschnigg, that Italy could no longer guarantee Austrian independence. In February 1938, von Schuschnigg paid Hitler a visit at Hitler's residence in Berchtesgaden in the Bavarian Alps, hoping to ease the tensions between their respective nations. The plan backfired as Hitler harangued von Schuschnigg with a list of grievances, and insisted that he appoint a number of Austrian Nazis into positions of influence (and benefit to Hitler), most notably Arthur Seyss-Inquart as Minister of the Interior. Non-compliance, Hitler warned, would result in military intervention. Faced with little choice, von Schuschnigg agreed. But the

Austrian chancellor, on his return to Vienna, announced a referendum on the issue of whether Austria wanted to remain independent or be incorporated into the German Reich. The date was set for March 13, 1938.

A furious Hitler ordered von Schuschnigg to cancel the referendum. Von Schuschnigg, having already lost the support of Mussolini, turned to France and Britain. There was nothing they could do. So, reluctantly, von Schuschnigg did as he was told and cancelled the referendum. Schuschnigg resigned and the Austrian president, Wilhelm Miklas, again under the threat of German intervention, appointed the Austrian Nazi, Seyss-Inquart, his successor. The following day, March 12, Seyss-Inquart "invited" Germany's army into Austria to help "restore order". The next day, Hitler announced the *Anschluss* (union) of Germany and Austria.

Immediately, Austria's Jews suffered. Forced out of their homes, their businesses closed, and liberties curtailed, the Jews were taunted and subjected to humiliation: the cleaning of pavements with toothbrushes or the hacking off of beards. Anti-Semitic laws were introduced, and some 30,000 Austrian Jews were rounded-up and sent to German concentration camps. Many managed to emigrate, while others, perhaps up to 10,000, committed suicide.

Nazi troops welcomed into Salzburg during the Anschluss, March 1938. German Federal Archives.

The referendum was finally held – on April 10. But with the Nazis now in control, it took a brave person to vote against the proposed *Anschluss*. As a result, 99.7 per cent voted to ratify the union.

The Sudetenland

Having achieved his Austrian objectives, Hitler's mind now turned to Czechoslovakia. But there was a potential problem for Hitler – namely Britain and France. But France had already showed itself incapable of acting once Hitler had marched his troops into the Rhineland so it was reasonable to suppose they would do nothing again. Hitler knew that tackling Czechoslovakia as a whole might be too much so he decided to concentrate on the area of the Sudetenland, an area consisting of three million Germans.

On September 15, 1938, Neville Chamberlain, Britain's prime minister, visited Hitler at his home in Berchtesgaden and listened as Hitler proclaimed that Czechoslovakia was the "last major problem to be solved", and demanded that the Sudetenland be incorporated into the German Reich. For Chamberlain, a soldier of World War One, his priority was to avoid another war and if this meant giving into Hitler over a small territorial demand, then so be it.

Chamberlain relayed Hitler's demands to the Czechoslovakian president, Edvard Benes.

On September 22, Chamberlain returned to Hitler, pleased that he had averted war. But Hitler was now demanding more, namely the right to the immediate occupation of the Sudetenland and that the

Czechoslovakian army leave the Sudetenland by October 1. Convinced that neither Britain nor France would intervene, Hitler threatened military action if his demands were not met.

A stalemate had been reached and war seemed a distinct possibility. Mussolini then stepped in as mediator and suggested a conference between himself, Hitler, Chamberlain and the French prime minister, Edouard Daladier, to thrash out the crisis. Edvard Benes was not invited.

The four men met in Munich on September 29. Chamberlain and Daladier yielded to Hitler's demands on condition that Hitler made no further territorial demands – which would secure the rest of Czechoslovakia. Hitler, delighted, agreed and the "Munich Agreement" was signed. Hitler and Chamberlain also signed a declaration of Anglo-German friendship, as "symbolic of the desire of our two peoples never to go to war with one another again".

Benes protested but no one took any notice. Anyway, he knew neither Britain nor France would risk war against Germany for the sake of the Sudetenland. Chamberlain returned to Britain, waving a piece of paper in his hand, declaring that the Munich Agreement had guaranteed "peace for our time".

The Munich Agreement, September 29, 1938. German Federal Archives. Front row, L- R: Neville Chamberlain, Édouard Daladier, Adolf Hitler, Benito Mussolini and Galeazzo Ciano.

Two days after the conference, on October 1, the German army marched into the Sudetenland. Five days later, under German pressure, Benes resigned, to be replaced by Emil Hacha.

Kristallnacht

On November 7, 1938, 17-year-old Herschel Grynszpan walked into the German embassy in Paris and demanded to see an embassy official. He was led to Ernst Vom Rath. Grynszpan shot him five times, fatally wounding him.

Joseph Goebbels, Hitler's propaganda minister, used the assassination as an excuse to launch a nationwide pogrom of Germany's Jewish population. On the night of November 9/10, Nazis throughout Germany and Austria went on the rampage, beating up Jews, breaking into their homes and terrorizing them, vandalising, looting and burning Jewish shops and businesses and violating Jewish cemeteries and synagogues. The sound of breaking glass gave the pogrom its nickname – the "Night of Broken Glass", or *Kristallnacht*. Almost 100 Jews were killed and 30,000 arrested and imprisoned in concentration camps. The following day, Hermann Goring held the Jews responsible for their own destruction and ordered the Jewish community to pay the German treasury a fine of 1 billion reichsmarks.

Legislation against the Jews intensified following *Kristallnacht* – Jews were banned from owning cars, from going to the cinema and theatre, and Jewish children were expelled from schools and universities.

Czechoslovakia

Meanwhile, Hitler was far from satisfied with the outcome of Munich: he'd got the Sudetenland but the complete annexation of Czechoslovakia was still the objective. On

March 15, 1939, Hitler summoned Emil Hacha to Berlin and, threatening to bomb Prague, insisted Hacha allow the entry of German troops into Czechoslovakia. The provinces of Bohemia and Moravia were to become Reich protectorates and Slovakia was to become an independent state, allied to Germany. Such was the shock, Hacha suffered a heart attack. Knowing, like Benes before him, he had no choice, Hacha relented. Hitler acted immediately and on that same day, German troops entered Prague. This time there were no cheering crowds. The people of Czechoslovakia knew that they had been invaded. Again, as in Austria eighteen months earlier, the new rulers immediately enforced anti-Semitic laws.

Hitler's invasion of Czechoslovakia shocked the British and French governments. They had been prepared to appease Hitler while he laid claim on behalf of German subjects and German speakers – the Rhineland, Saar, in Austria and the Sudetenland. But Hitler had no right to invade Czechoslovakia. Appeasement was dead and Hitler was not a man to trust.

Poland

Hitler's attention now turned to Poland. The Treaty of Versailles had cut the German province of East Prussia from the rest of Germany by a stretch of land known as the Polish Corridor. At the end of this corridor, on the Baltic coast, was the former German port of Danzig, now declared a "free city". Hitler now demanded the return of Danzig and the construction of road and rail links through the Polish Corridor. The Polish government refused. On March 31, the British and French governments, realising Poland's vulnerability, offered Poland the guarantee that if attacked, they would come to her aid. But in reality, neither Britain nor France had the military means to honour such a guarantee.

Nazis enter Czechoslovakia, March 1939.
German Federal Archives.

On May 22, 1939, Germany and Italy sealed their alliance with the "Pact of Steel", signed by their respective foreign ministers – Joachim von Ribbentrop and Galeazzo Ciano (Mussolini's son-in-law). The two nations agreed, amongst other things, on mutual assistance in the case of war.

The Pact of Steel caused Great Britain and France concern but it was the signing of another pact, three months later, that sent shockwaves throughout the world. On August 23, 1939, Nazi Germany and Bolshevik Russia, two ideological opponents that had never hidden their hatred of each other, signed a pact of non-aggression, the Molotov-Ribbentrop Pact, named after the two foreign ministers who signed it. Hitler, planning his invasion of Poland, wanted to avoid a war against the Soviet Union, and a war on two fronts as Germany had had to confront during World War One.

With a potential conflict against the Soviet Union now averted, Hitler was free to pursue his ambitions against Poland. On September 1, at 04.45, German troops launched their attack on Poland.

Poland turned to France and Great Britain and the guarantees signed six months before. Britain demanded that Hitler withdraw his troops from Poland. Hitler, of course, did not, hence at 11.15 on the morning of

September 3, Chamberlain announced that Britain had declared war on Germany. Six hours later, France followed suit.

War

Wanting to avoid the stalemate of the previous war, Hitler and his generals masterminded the technique of "lightning war", or Blitzkrieg. Air attacks, bombers and motorized infantry forged ahead and rapidly devastated the western provinces of Poland. As successive Polish towns and villages fell to the German army, SS squadrons followed up, rounding up and shooting citizens, burning villages to the ground and embarking on an orgy of killing and terror. Poland's Jewish population was particularly targeted and murdered.

On September 17, as secretly agreed in the Non-Aggression Pact, the Soviet Union launched their attack on Poland from the east. Neither Britain nor France were able to uphold the guarantees they'd made to Poland. Crushed between two totalitarian heavyweights, Poland buckled.

The end was swift. Warsaw surrendered on September 28.

Nazis invade Poland, September 1939. German Federal Archives.

Germany's triumphs during the first months of the war were spectacular. On April 9, 1940, Germany overran Denmark in a matter of hours.

On the same day, Germany attacked neutral Norway. Britain's attempts to intervene failed, resulting in Chamberlain's resignation. On May 10, he was replaced as prime minister by Winston Churchill. On the same day as Churchill became prime minister, Hitler launched his attack on the west. German forces entered neutral Luxembourg, Belgium and the Netherlands. Luxembourg surrendered within hours. The Netherlands surrendered on

May 14 and Belgium on May 28.

Hitler then ordered the invasion of France. The British Expeditionary Force and the French army were caught unprepared and were pushed back towards the English Channel. On June 10, with France's defeat assured, Mussolini, without invitation, joined the fight, keen to pick up the breadcrumbs of Germany's victory. On June 22, France surrendered and was to endure four years of Nazi occupation. Italy, for her part, was given a small 500-mile square pocket of French territory in the south-east.

On September 27, 1940, Germany, Italy and Japan signed the Tripartite Pact to "assist one another with all political, economic and military means" if any one of them were attacked by "a power at present not involved in the war". In November 1940, somewhat reluctantly, Hungary and Romania added their signatures to the Pact, followed in March 1941 by Bulgaria.

Within ten short months Poland, Denmark, Luxembourg, the Netherlands, Belgium and now France were under Nazi control. Hitler had reached the pinnacle of his rule. The relatively easily-won victories with comparatively modest casualties had won him much admiration in Germany. But the ultimate goal was the Soviet Union. Although plans were already under way, there was still unfinished business in the west; namely

Great Britain. On July 19, Hitler offered Britain the hand of peace – his "appeal to reason". Churchill rejected it out of hand.

Hitler knew that before he could launch an invasion of Britain, he would have to defeat the Royal Air Force. During the summer of 1940, the planes of the RAF and the Luftwaffe fought in the skies over southern England. On September 7, in response to a RAF raid on Berlin, the first German bombs fell on London. The Blitz had begun. The Battle of Britain continued, coming to a close at the end of October. The RAF held on. Hitler's planned invasion of Britain was to be postponed indefinitely.

The war spread rapidly. In March 1941, Germany's Afrika Korps began its offensive in North Africa, while on April 6, Germany invaded Yugoslavia and Greece.

But for Hitler, these were all mere preludes to his ultimate aim – the destruction of Bolshevik Russia. On June 22, he launched Operation Barbarossa, the invasion of the Soviet Union, the largest attack ever staged. Despite the vastness of Russian territory and manpower, Hitler anticipated a quick victory. And to begin with, this seemed entirely plausible. By mid-July, the Nazis had taken the Baltic States where they were initially welcomed as liberators from Soviet rule. Locals helped the roving teams of Nazi death squads, the *Einsatzgruppen*, to exterminate hundreds of thousands of Jews. Kiev in Ukraine fell in mid-September, resulting in half a million Soviet troops being taken prisoner. Outside Kiev, in the ravines of Babi Yar, on the September 29 and 30, the Nazi killing squads shot and killed 33,771 Jews.

German soldiers and a tank advance through Russia, June 1941. German Federal Archives.

By the end of August, Axis forces had cut off the Soviet city of Leningrad, subjecting the city to a siege that was to last almost 900 days to January 1944.

More and more Soviet cities fell to the Germans. By the end of October, Moscow was only 65 miles away; over 500,000 square miles of Soviet territory had been captured and, as well as huge numbers of Soviet troops and civilians killed, 3 million Red Army soldiers had been taken prisoner of war. But with the Russian winter at its most fierce and their supply lines stretched, the Germans were unable to advance and on December 5 had to abandon their plans to attack Moscow.

On December 7, 1941, Japan attacked the US fleet moored at Pearl Harbor on the Hawaiian island of Oahu. The effect was to being the US into the war. Four days later, on December 11, Hitler declared war on the US. Both acts, the invasion of the Soviet Union and the declaration of war against the US, stand up as Hitler's two greatest blunders. Germany's fate was sealed and the conflict, that had started 27 months before, was now truly global.

During 1941, the Nazis had come to the conclusion that the killing of Jews on the edges of pits was too time-consuming and detrimental on the mental health of the murder squads. Seeking alternative methods, the Germans began experimenting with gas, using carbon monoxide in mobile units or, from December 1941, at the first extermination camp, Chelmno, thirty miles from Łódź in Poland. Although an "improvement", this was still considered too slow and an inefficient means of mass murder. The use of Zyklon B gas on 600 Soviet prisoners-of-war in Auschwitz in September 1941 proved to be more rapid and efficient. On January 20, 1942, fifteen men representing various agencies of the Nazi apparatus met in a grand villa on the banks of Berlin's Lake Wannsee. The meeting, chaired by the chief of the security police and deputy to Heinrich Himmler, Reinhard Heydrich, discussed escalating the killing to a new, industrial level, what they referred to as the "Final Solution of the Jewish Question".

On February 15, 1942, the first transport of Jews from Upper Silesia arrived in Auschwitz, all of them were gassed on arrival.

On June 28, 1942, Hitler launched Operation Blue in order to capture the vital Russian oil fields in the Caucasus and the city of Stalingrad on the River Volga. Led by the Sixth Army, Germany's largest wartime army, commanded by General Friedrich Paulus, the Germans were fully expecting a total victory as they pushed the Soviet forces back. By August 23, the German advance had reached the outskirts of Stalingrad. Entering the city, the Germans, along with their Axis comrades, comprising of Italians, Romanians and Hungarians, fought the Soviets street for street, house for house, sometimes room for room.

But the Soviets organised an efficient counterattack. In desperate conditions, lacking food and medical supplies, and with temperatures plummeting, the Germans tried to hold on. Paulus sought Hitler's authority to surrender. Hitler forbade it. But on January 31, 1943, Paulus did surrender.

Captured German soldier, Stalingrad, January 1943.
German Federal Archives.

Germany's defeat at the Battle of Stalingrad was a bitter blow for Germany. Following his run of spectacular victories in 1940, Hitler's standing had been sky-high. Not any more. By the start of 1943, people were quietly beginning to question his leadership. On May 13, Axis forces in North Africa surrendered. Germany's defeat at the Battle of Kursk, east of Moscow, in July, confirmed for many that the war was now unwinnable. By the end of the year, Stalin's Red Army was recapturing towns and villages that had, two years before, fallen to the Germans.

RAF's Bomber Command had bombed strategic targets within Germany from as early as May 1940, but from 1942, the RAF and its American equivalent stepped up its campaign, targeting cities and major towns. In July 1943, a bombing raid over Hamburg killed over 40,000 civilians. The German Luftwaffe seemed incapable of preventing these attacks.

On July 10, 1943, Allied troops landed on Sicily. Mussolini was disposed and arrested. On September 3, the same day that Allied troops landed in southern Italy, Italy signed an armistice and, five days later, swapped sides and joined the Allies. On October 13, Italy declared war on Germany, its former ally.

On June 6, 1944, the Allies launched Operation Overlord, the invasion of Nazi-occupied France. Landing on five beaches on the Normandy coast, the Allies pushed the Germans further and further back. On August 25, Paris was liberated, followed on September 3 by Brussels. On September 10, US troops liberated Luxembourg. On the same day, at the German-Dutch-Belgium border town of Aachen, Allied troops set foot on German soil for the first time since the beginning of the war.

German prisoners of war, June 6, 1944. Imperial War Museum.

Meanwhile, on July 20, 1944, a clique of German officers, hoping to make peace with the Allies and save Germany from further destruction, tried to assassinate Hitler at his "Wolf's Lair" headquarters in Rastenburg, East Prussian. The plot failed.

On October 23, Soviet troops entered East Prussia and November 4 saw the surrender of Axis forces in Greece. On December 16, 1944, Hitler launched a last-ditch counter-offensive through the Ardennes forest in Belgium. Despite some initial success in what became known as the Battle of the Bulge, the Germans soon lost the impetus and the Allies, having suffered grievous losses, surged forward again.

German forces were surrendering everywhere and the German population suffered under continued and ever-effective bombing raids. On February 13, 1945, the east German town of Dresden was obliterated. By now only the most fanatical of Nazis believed that victory could still be theirs. They put their belief in the "wonder weapons" that Hitler had ordered. The new weapons were indeed effective – the V1 and V2 rockets. But their introduction came too late in the war to alter its outcome.

Liberation of prisoners at Auschwitz, January 1945.

The Soviets, advancing rapidly from the east, came across Hitler's death camps. The first to be liberated, on July 23, 1944, was Majdanek, on the outskirts of the city of Lublin. Other camps soon followed – Belzec, Sobibor and Treblinka amongst others. Then on January 27, 1945, the Soviets liberated Auschwitz.

In January 1945, with the Soviet Red Army bearing down on Germany, Hitler left his HQ in East Prussia and moved back to Berlin and into the Reich Chancellery. A month later, he went underground into the Chancellery's air-raid shelter.

On April 27, 1945, Mussolini tried to make his escape into neutral Switzerland. But he was discovered and the following day was executed.

Hitler's staff implored the Fuhrer to make good his escape but Hitler had no intention of fleeing and risking the chance of falling into Soviet hands. On April 30, Hitler committed suicide.

On May 2, Berlin surrendered. On May 7, Germany surrendered to the western Allies, and, the following day, to the Soviet Union.

The war in Europe was at an end.

Post-War

Immediately, the victorious allies began the work of peace. Germany lay in ruins. Up to 20 million civilians across Europe had lost their homes and had to be temporarily housed in one of the thousands of "displaced person camps". The Allies interviewed Germans and Austrians from all walks of life in a process called "de-Nazification", the means to prevent any remaining Nazi believers from regrouping or spreading their influence. Of course, very few still admitted to being a Nazi, and most went to great lengths to hide their Nazi pasts. The Allies fully intended to punish those deemed guilty of war crimes. But there were simply too many to cope with thus only the most senior and very worst offenders were put on trial.

The Nuremberg Trials, presided over by American, Soviet, British and French judges, began in mid-1945. 177

Germans and Austrians were put on trial: 25 were sentenced to death, 20 to life imprisonment, 97 imprisonment and 35 acquitted. It was no coincidence that Nuremberg had been chosen to host the trials – the city had been deeply associated with the Nazi Party, and the Allies wanted to symbolically emphasise the death of Nazism.

Nuremberg Trials. Defendants in their dock, 1946.
Front row, L – R: Hermann Göring, Rudolf Hess Joachim von Ribbentrop ana Wilhelm Keitel.

The trials were often criticized, both then and since, as victors' justice. The principal trial, lasting from November 1945 to September 1946, tried 21 senior Nazi leaders. 11

were sentenced to death. On October 15, 1946, on the eve of execution, Hermann Goring "cheated" the executioner by committing suicide. Thus ten were executed on October 16, including Joachim von Ribbentrop and Arthur Seyss-Inquart. Rudolph Hess was sentenced to life imprisonment and indeed died in prison in 1987. Franz von Papen was acquitted. Joseph Goebbels committed suicide the day after Hitler on May 1; Heinrich Himmler on May 23.

In 1934, Hitler declared that in the "next thousand years there will be no other revolution in Germany". This gave the expression the "Thousand-Year Reich". In the event, having caused suffering on a scale never seen before, having caused the most destructive war in history, and having inflicted the worst genocide in history, the Third Reich had survived just 12 years.

On October 10, 1945, the Nazi Party was officially abolished.

Nazi Germany: Timeline

October 1918   Start of the 'German Revolution'

Nov 9, 1918   Friedrich Ebert proclaims Germany a
republic

Nov 10, 1918   The German Kaiser, William II,
abdicates

Nov 11, 1918   Germany's defeat and the end of the
First World War

January 5-12, 1919 Spartacists, German communists,
stage an uprising in Berlin

January 19, 1919   First German democratic elections

August 11, 1919   Weimar Republic constitution ratified

June 28, 1919   Treaty of Versailles signed in the Hall
Of Mirrors

Sep 12, 1919   Hitler attends a meeting of DAP, the

German Workers' Party

February 24, 1920 DAP becomes the National Socialist German Workers' Party

July 29, 1921 Hitler becomes leader of NSDAP

January 11, 1923 French and Belgium forces occupy the Ruhr

November 8, 1923 The Munich *Putsch*, led by Hitler, fails.

April 1, 1924 Hitler is sentenced to five years but serves only eight months.

July 18, 1925 Hitler's autobiography, *Mein Kampf*, is published

July 1925 French and Belgium forces withdraw from the Ruhr.

Sep 10, 1926 Germany joins the League of Nations.

July 31, 1932 Reichstag elections – the Nazi poll almost 40% of the vote

January 30, 1933 Hitler appointed Chancellor within a coalition government.

February 27, 1933 The Reichstag Fire

March 20, 1933 Dachau, the first concentration camp, is opened.

March 23, 1933 Passing of the Enabling Act

April 26, 1933 The Gestapo, the Nazi secret police, is
formed

May 10, 1933 25,000 'un-German' books burned
across Germany

Jun 30-Jul 1, 1934 'Night of the Long Knives'

August 2, 1934 President Hindenburg dies.

January 13, 1935 Saar Plebiscite – 90.3% vote to rejoin
Germany

Sep 15, 1935 Nuremberg Race Laws come into
effect

March 7, 1936 German Army enters the Rhineland

July 17, 1936 Start of the Spanish Civil War

August 1, 1936 Start of the Berlin Olympic

October 19, 1936 Germany withdraws from the League
of Nations

October 25, 1936 Signing of the Rome-Berlin axis

Nov 25, 1936 Germany and Japan sign an anti-
Comintern pact.

April 26, 1937 The *Luftwaffe* bomb the Basque town
of Guernica.

November 6, 1937 Italy joins Germany and Japan in the
Anti-Comintern Pact.

February 4, 1938 Hitler appoints himself Commander-
in-Chief of the armed forces.

March 12, 1938   German army enters Austria and *Anschluss* is declared the following day.

September 29, 1938 Munich Agreement signed

October 1, 1938   German army occupies the Sudetenland

November 9, 1938 *Kristallnacht* or the 'Night of Broken Glass'

March 15, 1939   German invasion of Czechoslovakia.

May 22, 1939   Germany and Italy sign the 'Pact of Steel'

August 23, 1939   Germany and Soviet Union sign the Non-Aggression Pact

World War Two

1939

September 1   Germany invades Poland – start of World War Two

September 3   Britain and France declare war on Germany

September 27   Surrender of Warsaw

1940

April 9	Germany invades Denmark and Norway.
May 10	Germany invades Belgium, Holland and

Luxembourg.

May 15	Holland surrenders to Germany
May 27	Belgium surrenders to Germany.
June 10	Capitulation of Norway
June 22	France signs armistice with Germany
July 10	Battle of Britain begins

1941

March 30	German Afrika Korps begin offensive in

North Africa.

April 6	Germany invades Yugoslavia and Greece.
June 22	Operation Barbarossa – Germany invades

Soviet Union

December 11 Germany declares war on USA.

1942

August 22 Stalingrad offensive begins.

1943

February 2   German surrender at Stalingrad.

May 13   Axis forces in North Africa surrender.

October 13   Italy declares war on Germany.

1944

June 6   Operation Overlord – Allied invasion of
Normandy

July 20   Attempted assassination on Hitler.

August 25   Allies liberate Paris

September 3   Allies liberate Brussels.

October 23   Soviets enter East Prussia

1945

January 27   Soviets liberate Auschwitz.

April 23   Soviets enter Berlin

April 30   Hitler commits suicide.

May 7   German unconditional surrender to the
West.

May 8   German unconditional surrender to the
East.

Images

All the images used in this book are, as far as the publisher can ascertain, in the public domain. If they have mistakenly used an image that is not in the public domain, please let them know at felix@historyinanhour.com and they shall remove / replace the offending item.

CPSIA information can be obtained
at www.ICGtesting.com
Printed in the USA
BVHW041848080920
588243BV00002BA/517